Other books by Eric Sloane available as Dover reprints

A Museum of Early American Tools
American Barns and Covered Bridges
American Yesterday
A Reverence for Wood
Look at the Sky and Tell the Weather
Our Vanishing Landscape
Diary of an Early American Boy: Noah Blake 1805
The Seasons of America Past
The Cracker Barrel
Once Upon a Time: The Way America Was
Eric Sloane's Weather Book
Recollections in Black and White
Return to Taos: Eric Sloane's Sketchbook of Roadside Americana
Skies and the Artist: How to Draw Clouds and Sunsets
Eric Sloane's Book of Storms: Hurricanes, Twisters and Squalls
For Spacious Skies

(Log on to **www.doverpublications.com** for more information.)

The Little Red Schoolhouse

The LITTLE RED Schoolhouse

by ERIC SLOANE

DOVER PUBLICATIONS, INC., MINEOLA, NEW YORK

Bibliographical Note

This Dover edition, first published in 2007, is an unabridged republication
of the work originally published in 1972 by Doubleday and Company, Inc.,
Garden City, New York.

International Standard Book Number
ISBN-13: 978-0-486-45604-1
ISBN-10: 0-486-45604-8

Manufactured in the United States of America
Dover Publications, Inc., 31 East 2nd Street, Mineola, N.Y. 11501

Author's Note

The difference between yesterday's schoolhouse and that of today might seem to be merely the difference between two kinds of architecture and the difference of size. The real difference, however, is the simple difference between yesterday and today, and the way we live it. Education, like modern everyday life, has suddenly become regarded as a means of making more money. Startling as it sounds, life's values have become all too linked with the dollar, and the diploma is openly regarded as a guaranteed bank account. School days, like our everydays, have changed.

Living has lost tranquility—wars have become almost constant, strikes are part of daily work and rebellion is a popular school study. Normal education in this modern chaotic time often resembles a child trying to do homework while parents quarrel: students feel called upon to leave their orderly routine of study and try to patch up the confusion.

In a sense, this book is a ghost story of a less-troubled past. Dead and gone is that obsolete world of the early American one-room schoolhouse, yet it still haunts those who are old enough to recall it. There seems to be an ever-lingering spirit in most ancient places of learning, somewhat like that divine spirit that sets the solemn and proper mood in an old-time church.

Not long ago as I contemplated putting my sketches and notes about early schoolhouses into book form, I walked to the tiny red-brick school-house a mile from my studio in Warren, Connecticut. The door was open and I went inside. The place has been renovated many times during the last century I suppose, yet as I sat at one of the little desks I sensed a heavy yet not unpleasant presence of the past. The room had not been used since the lives and deaths of countless scholars, yet there was an unexplainable feeling that children had just left and would soon return. An aura of yesterday lingered there.

As my hand felt the surface of the initialed desk, there was an urge to carve my own initials there. I noticed a tiny tattoo-like spot under the skin on the back of my hand, the result of having tested the sharpness of an inked pen on my very first day of school. That was sixty years ago, but all of a sudden I recalled the incident clearly.

In my day, I remembered, most schoolboys carried pocketknives which were called "penknives." Later I learned that these penknives were originally

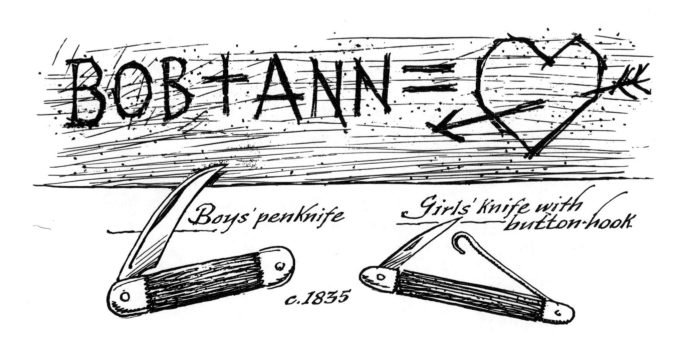

Boys' penknife

Girls' knife with button-hook

c.1835

used for making quill pens and that they were a necessary part of early American school equipment. Which seems to explain why the old desks were so carved with knifed initials. This desk was an almost solid pattern of bygone thoughts. One gem simply said, "Mary is a pip," and I'll bet she was! Another scratched note said, "Last day of school . . . 1846."

Historic shrines evoke nostalgia, but the old-time schoolhouse has a most particular ability to parade childhood memories, and I decided it was worth a book.

It seems worthwhile reviving any kind of spirit at all in this modern world so starved for lore and lacking in individual spirit: classrooms now have become more like business offices than halls of learning. Perhaps, I thought, the ghosts of yesterday's little red schoolhouse might be welcome companions. When Emerson said, "Only spirit can teach," he meant there must be an inner spirit (inspiration) for proper teaching and learning. Those old one-room schoolhouses were certainly overflowing with that.

The introduction to schooling is always a delicate, poignant and memorable performance for it is also the introduction to adulthood. In his autobiography, William Allen White recalled his first day of school. "What a day!" he wrote. "Ma started to take me but Pa objected. He always objected when she coddled me. Of course I like to be coddled, and I sided with her; but Pa had his way. The compromise was that he said, 'I'll take him.' And so we started out. Ma was in the doorway and I left her full of tears, for she knew, having taught school, that I would never come back her baby. She knew that I was gone out of her life as a child and would return that noon a middle-aged person, out in the world for good and all.

"Pa took me two blocks on my way to the schoolhouse, still three blocks away, and when he was out of sight of Ma in the doorway, he prodded me with his cane in pride and affection and said, 'Now, Willie, you are a man. Go to school!' and he turned and left me. He could not bear the shame of bringing me into the school-room, shame for him and shame for me, and we both knew it. And I trudged on."

As I sat at a desk of the Warren red-brick schoolhouse and closed my eyes, I tried to recall my own first school days. It was more difficult to remember the actual classrooms than it was to feel again the way I thought

Red Brick Schoolhouse 1784 at Warren, Connecticut

and the fresh experiences of youth. The only recollection of my first class-room was a painted motto that was framed and hung over the teacher's desk. It read: WHAT YOU ARE TO BE, YOU ARE NOW BECOMING. Half a century later those thought-provoking words continue to affect me.

I suppose there are still a few one-room schoolhouses in the remote stretches of America's West and Southwest. I recall (while working in the wheat fields as a boy) going to the "end-of-the-term box-lunch and spelling bee" of such a school in the Oklahoma Panhandle. Ladies brought boxes of food that were auctioned off to anxious dining partners, and the proceeds went to pay the salary of the school's bus driver. Children usually rode a pony or horse out to the highway, tethered the animal and then picked up the bus the rest of the way to school.

I remembered the spelling bee for grown-ups and how most parents hid or were embarrassed at not being able to spell simple words: one old cowpoke was caught sneaking out on his hands and knees, his rifle held in one hand, clanking over the floorboards. He was pulled back into the competition, but in the middle of the performance, word came about a break in a barbwire cattle fence. It broke up the adult spelling bee, and most of the male participants were glad to leave what they considered an ordeal.

While people overpopulate big cities and overcrowd the schools, most village schoolhouses are abandoned and children are taken by bus to huge modern buildings. At the time of writing this, there is a one room schoolhouse on Cape Cod; there is no schoolbus on Cuttyhunk Island. Last year there were three students left at the Cuttyhunk public school but two left after their eighth grade and eleven year old Claudia Jenkins became the class of one. Each day the flag is raised and a bell sounds at nine. Her two teachers (Harry and Caroline Cooper) are both of retirement age but they remain dedicated educators to the tiniest class in America.

There are not many haunted one-room schoolhouses left now, I suppose; some are rotting on back country roads and a very few have been preserved as quaint antiquities. But rather than battlefields or museums for the student of Americana, if he could visit those ancient schools, he might better feel the presence of our history. Helen Keller sat sightless at an old school desk and ran her fingers over its surface. "Here is American history," she later wrote. "It is not possible for civilization to flow backwards while there is still youth in the world."

ERIC SLOANE
Warren, Connecticut

The Little Red Schoolhouse

The HEART(H) of the Home

The disappearance of the old-time great fireplace is sad; it was the favorite American family gathering place. Now we gather about the TV set, but there is little or no contact or even conversation among a family watching a TV show. The hearth was once exactly what the word meant—the "heart" of the home, the center of communication.

Just off the kitchen fireplace in most early farmhouses was the "borning room." It wasn't reserved entirely for births, although families were so large then, I am sure the little room was a busy place in its own right. There, behind the wall-sized fireplace where it was warm and near the kitchen chores of the day, children saw the first light of day; and later started their lessons in reading and writing. I found my earliest example of the schoolroom blackboard (a six-foot-long by thirty-five-inch-wide blackened pine board) on the wall of a Vermont farmhouse borning room. When slate was being used only for roofing, the first "blackboards" were exactly that—black *boards,* or slabs of wood blackened with a mixture of egg white and the carbon of charred potato. Some of the old writing could still be seen, scratched by all-too-hard chalk (unrefined chalkstone): one line was probably put there by some teacher-mother over two centuries ago. It read: TIME IS SHORT. For them it certainly was.

In a wall cabinet of this borning room, I found a well-worn booklet named *The Mother's Primer.* Each page showed words with illustrations, with fine print below instructing the adult. "Point to the picture," one page read, "and say 'What is that?' Now ask the child to say the word over and over again. Now point to the word and sing it as in song, encouraging the child to do the same."

The little book, as shown herewith, promised to prepare the child for

the Mother's Primer.
c. 1830

school. "The author cannot but hope," it says, "that this book will enable many a mother or aunt, or elder brother or sister, or perhaps a beloved grandmother, by the family fireside, to go through in a pleasant and sure way with the art of preparing the child for his first school days."

Every now and then you will hear, while commenting upon how well things used to be built, that time-worn phrase, "those old-timers had all the time in the world!" This common misinformation is very sad because the old-timers actually had so *little* time. Even their life expectancy was less; without modern timesavers, electricity, lighting and ready-made materials, construction took as much as twenty times longer. Work days (without proper illumination) were nearly half as long. Even before starting work, the average man did primary house chores equal to a modern man's full day's labor.

Boys then had less time for schooling, attending only during the winter when there was less outside farm work. The winter term began the day after Thanksgiving and lasted from twelve to sixteen weeks. Girls, likewise, went to school when there was less indoor housework—their summer term starting the first Monday in May. Those pioneers did well for so little time available.

Mixed classes were at first only for very young boys and girls. A sort of advanced kindergarten, they were taught by women and known as

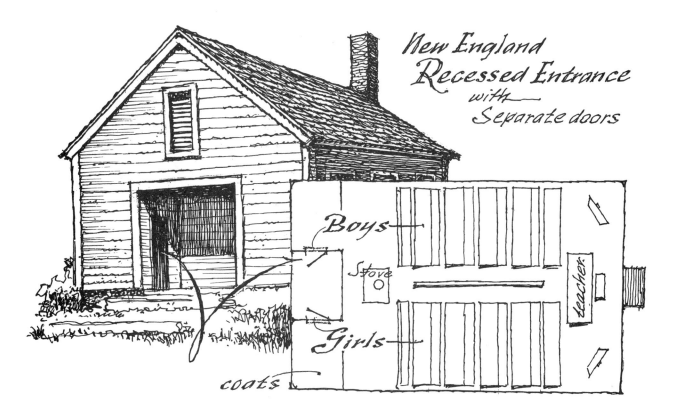

New England Recessed Entrance with Separate doors

"dames" in "dame schools." It wasn't until the 1800s that mixed grammar school classes were introduced, and then, as in Shaker Meetinghouses, the room was separated by a partition, with the girls on one side and the boys on the other. There were even separate entrances—one for girls and the other for boys—both in one recessed doorway.

The earliest school buildings were often makeshift outbuildings, unused barns, chicken coops and wagon sheds. One abandoned Cape Cod windmill, with its inner machinery removed, served as a schoolhouse for several decades. One school was held in a room over a stone well house at the John Chad Homestead in Chadd's Ford, Pennsylvania, where it still stands as a monument.

Most old county maps indicate all the houses with the names of the owners, and you might be surprised at the number of schoolhouses (usually marked as "S.H.") in any one area. This indicates that the early one-room

1790
old abandoned windmill on
Cape Cod used as a
Schoolhouse

schoolhouses were so scattered that students seldom walked more than a mile. An 1850 map of my own village (Warren, Connecticut) shows seven schoolhouses within an area of a two-mile circle; the present-day Warren school now serves an area of over fifteen miles, only possible, of course, because of the motor bus. It becomes evident that a great number of tiny one-room school buildings were not only adequate but because of their tininess were most efficient.

There is a New England legend about how some early schoolhouses had built-in watchtowers with spy windows, and one student always acted as a lookout against attacking Indians. Although this is completely untrue, there were such buildings, but they were none other than old abandoned town watchmen's houses. When the primitive practice of using town criers (who cried out each hour of the night) ended, their houses (indeed with watch rooms and spy windows) were left empty and available as schoolhouses. The

The Well-House School... Chadd's Ford, Pennsylvania.

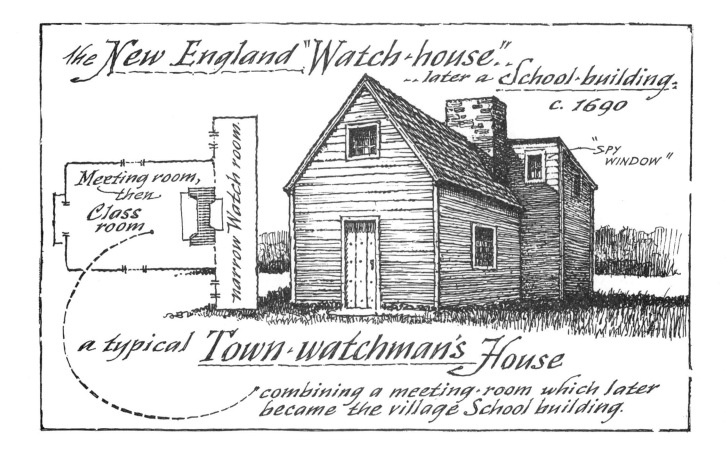

the New England "Watch-house"...
...later a School-building.
c. 1690

"SPY WINDOW"

Meeting room, then Class room

narrow Watch room.

a typical Town-watchman's House

combining a meeting-room which later became the village School building.

narrow watch room, I suppose, might have been used as living quarters for the schoolmaster; and so the "watchhouse school building" became Americana legend.

The idea of a school being within sight of the village was popular in the 1700s for safety reasons. Bears and wolves were common in Pennsylvania and New England, and they frequently roamed the streets during winter. One group of school children in New Hampshire in 1820 were returning from a late school party when they were attacked by a large bear. Six of the children managed to climb a tree only to watch the seventh, a small girl, devoured by the beast. When Indians attacked Deerfield, Massachusetts, Mrs. Hannah Beaman, the schoolmistress, and her flock were stationed in a remodeled stable, and with the Bible under her arm she led her class quickly —and just in time—to the fort. Those were rugged days indeed.

The original Massachusetts Colony passed a law requiring all parents to teach their children to read; five years later the law was changed requiring each township of fifty families to support a simple reading school, and each township of a hundred families to support a grammar school for "collidge preparement." College in those Puritan days, however, was primarily for those contemplating the ministry.

Going to "collidge" to become an early American minister might sound simple, but a properly educated man in those days was educated indeed. When Harvard began (only sixteen years after the landing at Plymouth), the requirements were many and severe. One was as follows:

> When any scholar is able to understand Tully or such like classical Latin author extempore, and make and speak true Latin in verse and prose . . . and decline perfectly the paradigms of nouns and verbs in the Greek tongue, let him then, and not before, be capable to admission into these halls.

There were eight other American colleges before the Revolution (all still operating) but their present-day entry requirements are in many ways simpler than in those pioneer days.

Connecticut Meeting House .. later, a Schoolhouse.
Thatched roof, squared logs.
"Cat and clay" chimney.
desks.
benches.
teacher

Vergennes (VERMONT) School — the schoolhouse built like a Church c. 1830

It is true that America's earliest schools were established for religious reasons, mainly so that children could read the Bible and quote from it. And there are those who now violently condemn this idea and criticize the early schools for having been overreligious. Yet without the available church buildings and the abandoned meetinghouses, the ministers who doubled as schoolmasters and the only available book which happened to be the Bible, there would have been a whole century in America without any schools at all. The Connecticut log meetinghouse with its thatched roof was a temporary church that immediately became a one-room schoolhouse as soon as a proper church was built. Many existing rural New England schools were once religious meetinghouses.

For over a century just off an old road south of Vergennes in Vermont, a remarkably beautiful school building, looking like a church, stood on land donated to the city by General Strong. He was a retired Revolutionary War officer with foresight and a sense of humor. The building, he stipulated, was to be rented at an annual rent of one kernel of Indian corn, payable on the first of each January.

Time came when the Vergennes brick school became too small for a bus-transported student body, and soon it stood rotting—a monument to a bygone age. In 1946 it was dismantled and put together again brick by brick, the first building to be moved to the then new Americana restoration at Shelburne, Vermont.

The one room of Vergennes' brick school is twenty-two by thirty feet, designed for thirty children, heated more by a room-length stovepipe than the tiny 1830 stove. The belfry hints of its having been designed originally as a church, but by any standards it is regarded as possibly being the handsomest one-room schoolhouse in America.

Schooling as we know it now would have been useless in Colonial primitive America; arithmetic (known then as the "art of cyphering") arrived

in the average classroom during the 1700s. In fact, the well-known "three Rs" (now representing "reading and 'riting and 'rithmetic") was originally "reading and 'riting and *religion*." It does seem a pity, or even a disgrace, that the Bible, which began American education and taught so many lessons of morality just as important as arithmetic, should now be banned from most of our schooling. It is, in my mind, bigotry in reverse.

With the closing of the Colonial period and the waning of Puritanism, schools began to teach more than just reading and writing, and finally there was less involvement with the Bible. But the job of teaching still lay heavily upon the church, sometimes simply for the want of a better source.

Going to school was often fun.

The first southern schoolhouses were log shacks erected in abandoned fields too full of rocks or too overcultivated for farm use and therefore not taxed. Such property was called an "old field." George Washington attended an old-field school presided over by an old-field master, who was a retired old-field minister from an old-field church. Even in those days, it appears, avoiding taxes was an important trick, and the term "old field" was the popular tax-exempt phrase of the day. George's seven-mile trip to school each day necessitated his rising at five in the morning. At twelve years of age he rowed across the river to a more advanced Fredericksburg teacher, and at thirteen his childhood education ended. But the long trips to school were far from being a boring chore for young Washington. Instead, he made a game out of surveying all the routes, and his first drawn plans as a student surveyor were the various trails to school.

"an old-field" School.
Virginia c. 1735

Log House

*the first School "desks"
and Benches*
were rough hewn boards along
the walls of a log-cabin.

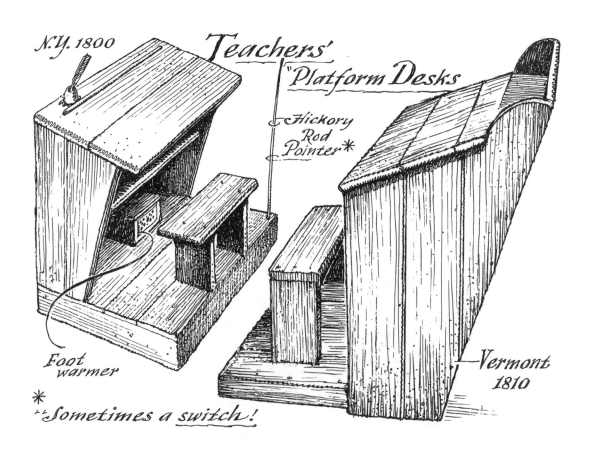

N.Y. 1800

*Teachers'
"Platform Desks*

Hickory
Rod
Pointer *

Foot
warmer

Vermont
1810

* Sometimes a <u>switch</u>!

New England schoolhouses were more centrally located, but like the southern old-field buildings, they were often constructed of logs. Instead of separate desks, sticks were driven between the logs in the wall at about a height of four feet and planks were then laid on top, like slanted shelves. Rough planks placed alongside, served as seats. School desks as we know them became standard in the 1800s.

The first American school desks were made of wood and were placed upon platforms to separate them from the tamped dirt floor to keep students' feet warmer during winter. One diary tells how, without a blackboard, lessons were sometimes scratched into the schoolhouse's dirt floor with a stick. Many accounts recall how unruly boys often scuffed the dirt into clouds of dust whenever the teacher left the room.

The master's desk was on a raised platform, too, at first with its bench attached. I found one such master's desk with a place for resting a birch-rod pointer (which I am sure doubled as a switch on occasion), and there were

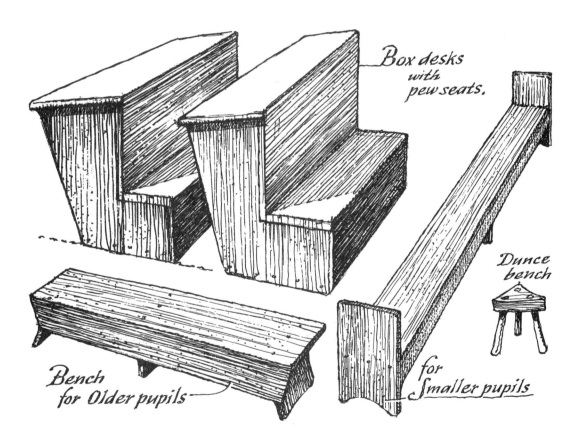

Box desks with pew seats.

Bench for Older pupils

Dunce bench for Smaller pupils

1761

a Foot-stove for standing upon.

PRESENTED TO YE REVEREND JOHN BOWER

burned marks beneath the desk proving that the teacher had at one time used a coal foot warmer.

I have never found evidence of school children using foot warmers, but I feel certain they did. One of my rarest finds was a special oversize foot warmer designed for *standing upon* that had been presented to a minister by his parish in 1761. But, along with several small foot warmers presumably used by students, I found it in the attic of a tiny schoolhouse where he had later taught.

In the same schoolhouse attic were several rusty old two-pound tobacco tins that had been used as lunch boxes. Back in the days when nothing was thrown away, lard, tobacco, dried fish and tea were sold in tins designed to later serve as school children's lunch boxes; some were even equipped with wooden handles. Nowadays you send in a box top and money to get some sort of premium, but in those days the container itself was the premium: flour was sold in printed calico dress goods' bags, blue dye came from the

NOON DAY EXERCISES

Tea
was sold
in this one

a four
Compartment box.

GIVE
THANKS
FOR
FOOD

1835

blue paper sugar was wrapped in, and tin cans were designed to last for years to come.

Heating the classroom was always a major problem. Sometimes with two fireplaces to feed, ten or twelve cords of wood would not last the winter, and the woodshed was frequently as large or even bigger than the schoolhouse itself. The woodshed was often a lean-to attached to the schoolhouse, but the most accepted arrangement was to place it between the schoolhouse and the privy, with a fence separating the boys' entrance from the girls'. The ancient designation of privy doors was to saw into them a sun (for boys' toilet) and a moon (for girls' toilet).

The students' parents were responsible for heating the old-time class-room, and the student who brought in the least wood usually sat farthest from the fire. It was a rule of the mid-1700s for each scholar to bring in one "load"

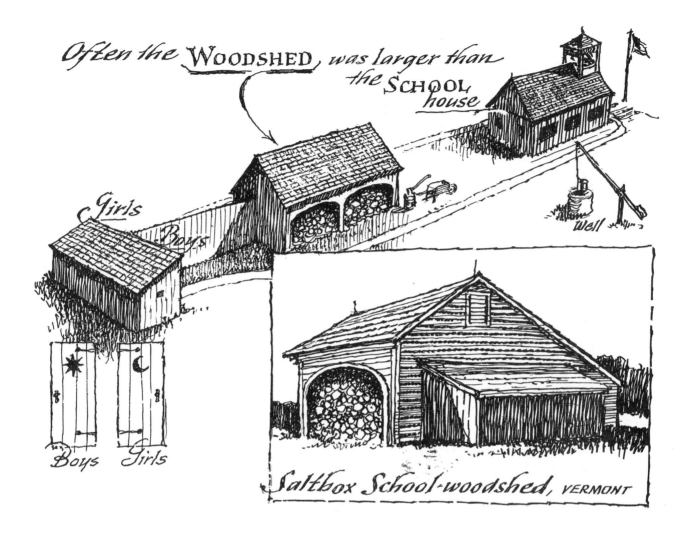

Often the WOODSHED, was larger than the SCHOOL house

Girls

Boys

Boys   Girls

Well

Saltbox School-woodshed, VERMONT

(half a cord) of good wood for the winter term. Although "in default thereof" the student was "subject to expulsion," a fine of six shillings was the general forfeit. As late as 1825 in Hartford, Connecticut, areas, the "out country" schools voted that: "Each scholar shall furnish ten feet of seasoned hardwood, or green walnut or white ash, to be inspected by the master. This wood to be delivered at commencement time, or a penalty of forty cents in money shall thereby be subjected." Each week a different boy, designated "fire-monitor," opened the schoolhouse, cleared out the spent ashes and started a new fire.

Earlier than most realize, the iron stove arrived on the American scene. But the "black box with a fire in it" was feared by many because it offered no exchange of fresh air for proper ventilation such as was present with an open fireplace. Particularly where many people were in a room all day, stoves were avoided; but by 1800 this fear lessened and both schools and churches admitted stoves to their interiors. Without fireplaces or stoves, churches were completely unheated.

The center stove usually needed a center chimney, and so the American round (and hexagonical) schoolhouse was born. The first examples were built in New Jersey and Pennsylvania, but the vogue spread throughout the country in the early 1800s. New York school board architects said, "the new hexagonical school building design built around a center stove is a model of fitness, with evenly distributed heat for all the class. Furthermore, windows in such a building may be placed overhead: light from above is far better and stronger than the light from the sides of a building, especially on cloudy days. The strong propensity which scholars have to look out by a side window would thereby be prevented. We foresee all schools in the United States being built hexagonically; the larger the school, the larger the hexagon."

It seemed like a good idea, and it happened at a time when the Shakers devised their round barns as models of agricultural fitness. But the hexagon building for a hundred students would have to be a big hexagon indeed; and the "school in the round" didn't appeal to teachers who liked to face their audience from one end of a room. So only about a hundred or so of them were built (a dozen or two such buildings remain), and the roundish school-house was soon forgotten. But they were probably the first completely original American architectural design: they were so different, in fact, that modern architects are now planning similar "new" round schoolhouses.

It seems strange that the one-room schoolhouse persisted for so long and separate rooms for separate grades appeared so late. Yet yesterday's multi-grade classroom students were not unlike today's youngsters as they listen in on adult-TV dialogue as much as sixty hours a week—even while doing their homework. It actually benefited the lower grades of the old-time one-room schoolhouse to be present during advanced-grade recitations,

The Octagonal Meeting-house of the 1700s became a suitable Schoolhouse.

New Jersey's "Old Harmony" in Raritan Township

Later (c. 1835) the design took shape with Sky Light illumination, as "the ideal Schoolhouse"..

— chimney

— glass windows

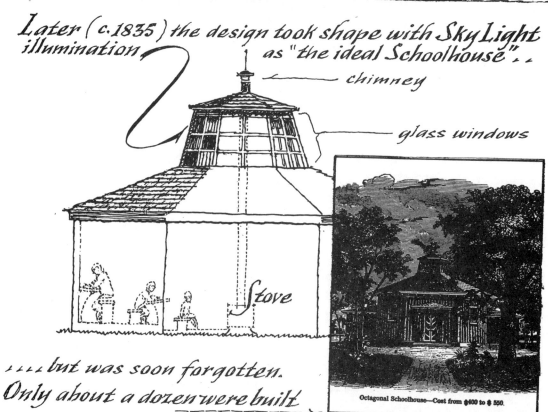

Stove

Octagonal Schoolhouse—Cost from $400 to $550.

....but was soon forgotten. Only about a dozen were built →

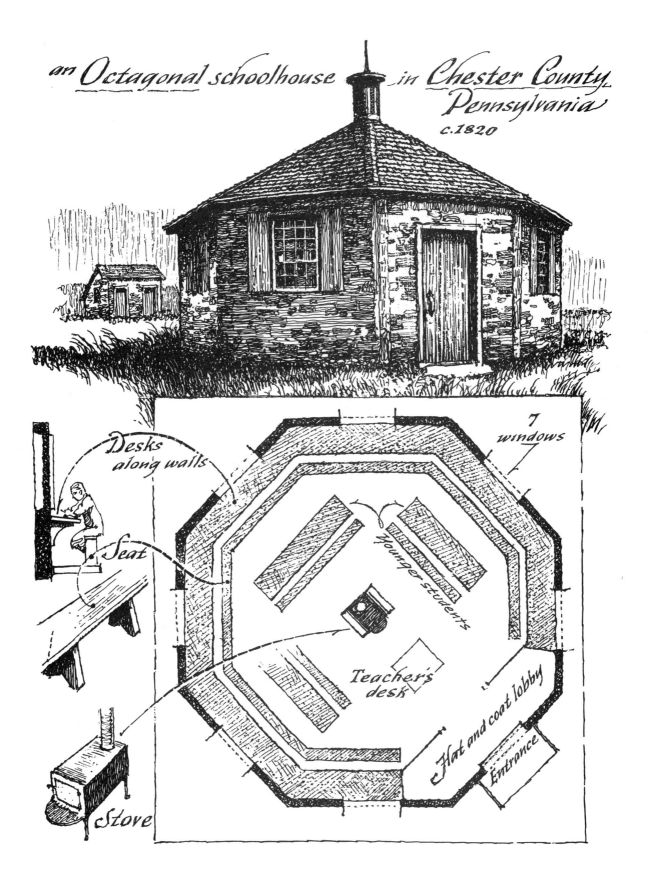

an *Octagonal* schoolhouse ...in *Chester County,* *Pennsylvania* c.1820

Desks along walls

7 windows

Seat

Younger students

Teacher's desk

Hat and coat lobby

Entrance

Stove

for the younger scholars were exposed to what they would be confronted with later on. Primitive as the arrangement was, the school also had the feeling of being one big family of children instead of being separated into groups of students who tend to regard themselves as either inferior or superior to the rest of the student body.

It should also be remembered that the one-room class occurred when apprenticeship was popular, when the novice worked alongside the master and there was a closer kinship between the learner and the expert. That sort of association develops a closer bond between mankind, which, I suppose, is an important lesson in itself.

American wartime heroes are well documented in history, but the quiet men who taught in pioneer schools were often greater heroes without mention. Patriotic and dedicated, with little or no thought of proper salary, some teachers asked no more than room and board for their services.

One young American graduated from Harvard at eighteen and decided to embark on a teacher's career. His first employment was in a tiny one-room schoolhouse at East Haddam, Connecticut, where at that time, in the fall of 1773, five dollars a month was considered fair pay as a schoolmaster's salary. He was so well liked that when he left the second year for another school in nearby New London, his students gave him a "school treat." This was a sort of send-off party at the end of the term, celebrated with a cider-and-molasses-and-water-and-vinegar drink called switchel. It was also the time when students brought in the cornmeal and produce of the farm that made up much of the schoolmaster's salary.

"I'll miss you," the departing schoolmaster said in a short speech, "and I wish that part of me could stay back here in East Haddam with you. I do regret there is only one of me!" He was quoting from a Greek classic which had been part of the school lessons during the year.

Shortly afterward as he stood on the gallows ready to be executed by the British as a spy, he made a similar remark. "I do regret," he said, "that I have only one life to give for my country." This utterance by schoolmaster Nathan Hale lives on in American history as the words of an outstanding soldier; but he was probably a better schoolmaster than he was a spy. The secret military plans of the British were found written in Latin and Greek,

Where Nathan Hale taught in 1773.

hidden in his shoe. Hale's little schoolhouse still stands at East Haddam today.

Most early American schoolmasters were churchmen dedicated to the community. They were often the ones who also tolled the bells, called meetings, doubled as choirmasters, read from the Bible and gave up notices to the preachers by sticking them in crotched poles and holding them up to the high pulpits. One schoolmaster of New Preston, Connecticut, was a retired minister who also taught "singing, painting, gilding and playing upon the organ." A teacher who opened grammar classes in Brooklyn, New York, had a card advertising himself as "master of grammar and writing, also comforter of the sick." When the sick died, he made a few shillings as village gravedigger. From the beginning, teaching seems to have been one of America's least profitable businesses and needed to be aided by outside work, which even in the early days was known as "moonlighting." They often taught by daylight and earned a living by moonlight.

...another "Oldest Wooden School Building"...
...this one in St. Augustine, Florida
...built of Red Cedar.

In 1768 the town of Litchfield, Connecticut, voted "to hire a grammar schoolmaster for a year as cheap as possible, to act as court messenger, to serve summons and to lead the Sunday choir. He must be a fit person, when called upon, to preach the word of God and to keep a tidy school." Although poorly paid, the schoolmaster was a dedicated American with a most honored place in the community, second only to the minister.

Teachers' salaries were as small in size as they were varied in medium. "Provision pay" included corn, flax, oats, hay, brick, iron and all sorts of farm produce. Before the Revolutionary War a master's salary averaged the equivalent of a dollar to a dollar and a half a week (besides bed and board), half in money and half in provision pay. In some cases salary was entirely in tobacco, which was auctioned off at the end of the term by the schoolmaster himself. In Dedham, Massachusetts, the master's salary in 1700 was "five pounds per quarter, half in wheat and half in other corn." Another record puts a Massachusetts teacher's salary as: "twenty pounds of sugar, sixteen yards of satin, three pecks of apples, three quarters of a lamb, three yards of red cotton, a fat cow, thirty pounds of butter and two thousand nails." Sometimes the most arithmetic involved with a teacher's work was confined to his own account book.

I recall reviewing a recent school history book for the New York *Times*. Each subject was given exactly one page: George Washington was given a page of three short paragraphs, but a completely crowded page was afforded to the first Negro killed in the Revolutionary War. It was evident that this book was written for the needs of today. But the three paragraphs "covering" early American education regarded it as almost worthless. One of these paragraphs was devoted to the "bigotry and extreme cruelty of early American schoolmasters."

I do find constant reference to how children used to be punished in school. It is true that the the hickory stick was a most important piece of schoolroom equipment and that some Puritan classrooms actually had whipping posts. But few of us stop to remember that this sort of horror was not confined to the school; instead, it was the common way of life. If Father swore on the Sabbath or Mother was known as a common scold, the ducking stool, the stocks or public whipping was the order of the day. Only a hundred and fifty years ago, for example, there were still in the United States lawbooks rules for punishing adultery. They consisted of burning the letter "A" on the foreheads of both the man and the woman involved, who were then forced to wear wooden halters around their necks whenever in public. Found without the halter, they were due for thirty lashes. It seems that chastisement was part of life and part of education, just as spanking a dog to housebreak him seems proper. "Spare the rod and spoil the child," was both household and classroom psychology.

Students were commonly struck across the hand with a ruler. But the early ruler (more correctly called a *ferula*) was not the hardwood stick we now know, used for measuring. It was a very light, flat, limber piece of wood used specially for chastising. It made a loud slapping sound but was designed not to injure. This ferula was the schoolmaster's emblem of authority, and when he left the classroom it was passed on to a monitor or special student elected to keep order in the room. The ferula happened to have a straight edge and therefore seemed a suitable instrument for making ruled lines on paper. There were no printed ruled papers in those days, and the ruled guide-lines were marked with lead (plummet pencils) during the spare time of both teachers and students. From this practice, the ferula became the heavy maple ruling stick with inches marked upon it, which we now call a ruler.

In a class where students ranged from four to seventeen years of age, there was room for a multitude of fancy juvenile mischiefs, and it seems almost inconceivable that any semblance of order and quiet was possible. Each punishment had to be carefully chosen as it affected the whole class audience. Girls were never spanked, but a simple rap on the palm with the ferula was considered proper. A more unruly girl might be made to sit in the corner or to sit for half an hour on a one-legged milking stool called the uniped. A boy's punishment was often none other than having to sit among the girls. But there were times when in the absence of a teacher the whole school met in complete disorder, and as one account related, "the master piled all the boys in a pyramid and spanked the unlucky ones on top."

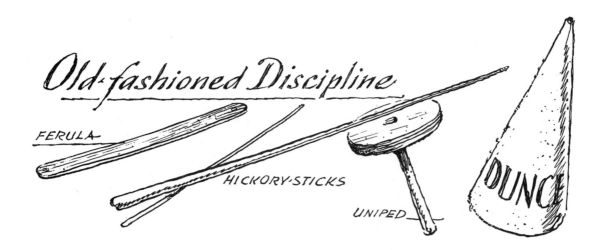

Old-fashioned Discipline

FERULA

HICKORY-STICKS

UNIPED

DUNCE

In early days, the word discipline did not refer to punishment as it now does, and it seems a pity that a respected word has become ugly and dreaded. Classroom discipline meant classroom rules, order, instruction, education and knowledge. Coming from the word "disciple," which meant "*a scholar, one who receives instruction from another,*" the old-time school was full of *disciples* who respected *discipline*.

Back in the 1700s a Franklin *Almanack* said, "Discipline in the classroom is as necessary as discipline on the highway." And as traffic increases and classrooms enlarge, it seems to me that discipline becomes more and more important. The early American philosopher Jonathan Edwards summed it up: "Education is what is given and gotten in college, discipline for life's duties, discipline to life's natural moral laws, discipline in the rule of life's Great Exemplar." They seemed to know exactly what they went to school for in those days, and it was much more than reading and 'riting and 'rithmetic. It was also to understand discipline.

A recent Vice-President of the United States said that "a man with a college degree will earn a hundred thousand dollars more during his lifetime than a man without a degree." And so, many children are being sent to college with the inspiration that they might get the best jobs and earn the most money; they are told that the dropout is destined to be a financial failure. It must be confusing when they learn that most of the richest men of our time had the least education, and the poorest paid are sometimes the teachers.

The old-time school was at least honest and specific in its aim to mold a better person with no thought about what money he might earn; I suppose that is one reason why so many lessons involved the Bible. Faith, hope, charity, love, decency, honesty, patience and humility were subjects for English composition and penmanship. Morality was an issue and a serious study.

The outdoor spaces around most schools nowadays look like used-car lots. The students most likely to succeed own the latest model sports cars; the rickety high-mileage cars usually belong to the teachers. Some do their studies as they are being bussed across the countryside, often knowing the bus drivers better than they know their teachers. The ways of childhood have

School slate-box

(closed)

open

CARDS

Moment Negate Omens
Revere School Turning
Vexing Wizard Youths

Valentine Hofmann

26436 31470 8909 369542
71529 20341 1044 180915
39050 67512 3209 603956
        5-1+3 9-9+5 6-2÷+3

abcdefg.

CARDS

suddenly become chaotic and accelerated; it seems sad that tomorrow's school-day recollections cannot be the slow, simple sort of rich childhood memories of yesterday.

Nowadays you hear of younger people "doing their thing" and rejoicing in a new-found expression of one sort or another. Actually, there is nothing new-found about it, for centuries ago people were often happier and more aware of life because everyone "did their thing"—making their clothing, raising and preparing their food and rejoicing at the end of the week by giving thanks to a God they believed in. Children started out doing their own things at their school; they made their own quill pens and lead pencils and they made their own rag-paper copy books at home. Sheets of "foolscap paper" were set aside for books that were cut, sometimes ruled and then sewed together into book form with a waxed thread. Foolscap was the name of a simple kind and size of folded writing paper that at one time was ornamented with the watermark design of a fool's cap and bells.

Lead pencils were originally rods of lead, not used for writing but just for making ruled lines on writing paper. The modern wood-covered carbon pencils (still bearing the ancient name of lead pencil) didn't arrive in America until the 1800s. The first pencil factory was opened in New York in 1860. The well-known pencil box of school days was preceded by a slate box, which was usually an elaborate affair, almost like a tiny desk. It held copying cards and writing materials and had a slanted hinged slate top. It is a mystery why so few of these still exist.

"Foolscap Copy-book
1814

Folded and sewed
Writing practice

Fellowship &c Contd

7 & b, B and C joind in company A's cloth is set for 12 months, B's
160 yards of cloth 8 months and C's 248 bushels of wheat 6 months
their gain is such that A and B's share is 456£ & and C's 471£
C and A's 375£. Required the whole gain each ones respectively
the price of B's cloth per yard and what C's wheat was per bush
Answer whole gain 631£ A's share 80£ B's 256£ and C's 175£
B's cloth 10s per yard and C's wheat 6s 2d per bushel

A & B = 456   631   631   631   A 100 256   50
B & C = 451   431   375   456   160   12
C & A = 375   4526 00B 256 C 175   600
         2)1262   256
whole gain 631   3600
A 80£ 175 50   1600 536 00 96
   700   600   1500   14400
             275   Bu £ Bushel   240   9600
            5000   A 240 75 . . 1   1440   2600
            4200   60
             200   240 720
    1400 150 00 175   720
          2800   60 100 . 95
          2100   1500
          2100   160 320 12 Bushel

Exam Exchange

Exchange is the rule by which the the money &c of one state or
country is reduced to that of another
Par is equal in value but the course of exchange is frequently
above or below par
Agio is a term used to signify the difference in some countries
between bank and current money

Case 1st Exchange between the United States

Case 2d March 12th D 1814

Foreign Exchang

Accounts are kept in England Ireland and the West
India Islands in pounds shillings pence and farthings
though their intrincic values in these places are different

A Table of different Monies

France		
12 Deniers	=	1 Sol
20 Sols	=	1 Livre
3 Livres	=	1 Crown
Spain		
4 Maravedies Vellon or	} =	1 Quarta
28 Maravedies of Plate		
8 Quartos or	} =	1 Rial Vellon
34 Maravedies Vellon		
16 Quartos or	} =	1 Rial of Plate
34 Maravedies of Plate		
8 Rials of Plate	=	1 Piastre Peso or Dollar
5 Pesos	=	1 Spanish Pistole
2 Spanish Pistoles	=	1 Doubloon
Italy		
12 Deniers	=	1 Sol
20 Sols	=	1 Livre
5 Livres	=	1 Piece of Eight at Genoa
6 Livres	=	1 Pitti at Leghorn
6 Solidi	=	1 Gross
24 Grosses	=	1 Ducat
Portugal		
400 Reas	=	1 Crusado
1000 Reas	=	1 Millrea

All paper was made of rags, and it was unheard of to throw away even
a piece of it. Ministers who wrote their sermons on this scarce and valuable
material wrote in a very tiny script and then carried the manuscript over to
the back of the page. School children never scribbled carelessly but wrote
from page edge to page edge (without margins), writing carefully and only
that which they intended to save. Each written lesson, therefore, found its
way into a sewn booklet kept for the whole term: not one piece of usable
paper was ever destroyed. How different now, when wood-based paper turns
yellow and rots in a few decades, and each person discards as much as a ton
of paper a year.

Good penmanship was taken for granted in the eighteenth century, and students spent many an hour practicing. The beautiful penmanship and the mastery of language and sentiment which these young people of two centuries ago achieved required remarkable diligence and ability. Everyone was expected to write well, but the writing master, especially, was known for his decorative flourishes. Although his business card was often simply a few words written with a quill pen, the samples he carried in his brochure were works of art. Often a simple bill of sale or letter of credit was embellished with decoration, so the art of flourishing was an important part of good penmanship.

The following 1740 form letter for a student to his father, suggests addressing Dad as "Honored Sir" and signing himself as a "most dutiful Son." The fact that such wording between father and son sounds ridiculous is not only indicative of our times but worth some profound thought.

Hon.ᵈ Sir, June 27.ᵗʰ 1740.

This is the sixth Letter I have sent you by divers Ships, since Michaelmas last; which are I hope, all come safe to hand. I have nothing new or particular to communicate, only beg you would conceive so favourable an opinion of me, as to believe I prosecute my Studies with the utmost application; well knowing, that will prove the best recommendation to your favour at present, and most real Service to my self in time to come. All our Friends here present their kind love to you, and that you may continue in health and happiness, is the constant prayer of

Your most dutiful Son.

I remember the writing practices I did in my own school days. One favorite sentence (because it contained all the letters of the alphabet) was, "The quick brown fox jumped over the lazy dog," but most practice sentences pertained to business quotations like, "Ninety days after date I promise to pay the sum of ten dollars." In the Colonial 1700s, however, all quotations and practice sentences were planned also to instruct or inspire morality. Alphabetically arranged, there were books containing such simple and suitable sayings as, "Affectation is odious" (A), "Banish evil thoughts" (B), "Cease to do evil" (C), etc. The collection of such sayings shown here-

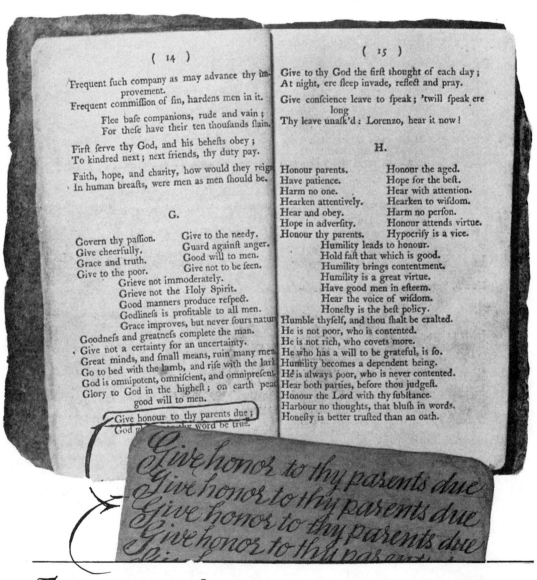

For penmanship practice, a good saying from the Bible.

with explains that they were collected in book form . . . "to rear the tender thought, and teach the young idea how to aspire."

The hand-written notations and comments written in ancient school-books are sometimes as revealing as the printed texts, usually giving proof of adult common sense and often an extraordinary sense of humor. Some chose to inscribe after their name, "Mark well this name, for I shall shame whoever steals and takes the blame." Another favorite was "Steal not my book for if you do, the Devil will be after you." Perhaps the oldest American flyleaf comment on record was written in 1640:

"God give me Grace to read and remember the truths herein."

Perhaps the rugged life and strict religious rules of colonial days caused children to be more serious about life and exacting in their learning: perhaps the easy living and absence of rules nowadays causes children to be lax. At any rate it is interesting and enlightening to compare yesterday with today. Consider one letter written by John Quincy Adams when he was in school at the age of nine years:

Braintree, June the 2nd, 1777.

Dear Sir: I love to receive letters very well, much better than I love to write them. I make a poor figure at composition, my head is too fickle, my thoughts are running after bird's eggs, play and trifles till I get vexed with myself. I have but just entered the third volume of Smollett 'tho I had designed to have got it half through by this time. I have determined this week to be more diligent. . . . I have set myself a stent and determine to read the third volume half out. If I can but keep this resolution, I will write again at the end of the week and give a better account of myself. I wish, Sir, you would give me some instructions with regard to my time and advise me how to proportion my studies and my play, in writing: I will keep them by me and endeavor to follow them. I am, dear Sir, with a present determination of growing better, yours,

John Quincy Adams.

P.S. Sir, if you will be so good as to favour me with a blank-book,

If such a letter is an indication of the typical child and his schooling in America two centuries ago, we might ponder the effects of modern day progress.

Nostalgia has no place in today's school: nostalgia is a kind of disease—a "dis-ease" with the present, and a desire to return into the past. But there were good things of the past which should be recognized and revived: this is *not* nostalgia.

The one-room schoolhouse is too much a part of America to be forgotten, and its lessons live on in the words of those who learned there as children and grew up to mold the nation. The little red schoolhouse did its job well.